13 Skyscrapers
Children Should Know

Brad Finger

PRESTEL

Munich · London · New York

Contents

Reaching for the sky

A skyscraper is no ordinary building. It can transform the look of an entire city, changing the way people live in that city and even how they feel about it. When you think of places like New York, Chicago, Hong Kong, or Dubai, you often picture the huge towers that make up those cities' skylines.

For thousands of years, people have tried to build structures that could touch the sky. The great pyramids of ancient Egypt were famous for their height, and they were the tallest buildings in the world for almost 4,000 years! In medieval Europe, elegant cathedral towers reached upwards toward heaven. But it wasn't until the late 1800s that the first true skyscrapers were built. They used the new technology of the Industrial Revolution:* steel-frame skeletons, elevators, and electric lights. At first, skyscrapers were designed as clean, quiet places where people could work—places set apart from the noisy, busy streets of the city. Over time, as skyscrapers became taller and more expensive to build, people began to rethink how to use them. Some of today's towers are built like miniature cities, with offices, hotels, and even gardens and parks within their gleaming walls.

In this book, you can learn about 13 of the world's most important and influential skyscrapers. Each chapter will discuss how these structures were built and how they helped transform their cities. Some of the words may be difficult to understand. So we've added an asterisk* to these words and defined them in a glossary at the back of the book.

At the top of each chapter, a timeline of events will tell you what was happening in the world when a particular skyscraper was built. You can also answer some quiz questions about what you read, and you will find tips for learning more about each tower. But most importantly, have fun on your journey to explore the tallest buildings on Earth!

Louis Sullivan 1856–1924

1857 First modern
elevator

1850s Water closets*
become popular

1825 Erie Canal in
New York completed

1861–65
American Civil War

1815   1820   1825   1830   1835   1840   1845   1850   1855   1860   1865   1870

Guaranty Building

The Guaranty Building
(now called the
Prudential Building)
stands proudly in
downtown Buffalo,
New York. Its thin,
elegant piers* stretch
upward, making the
building seem taller
than it really is.

Guaranty Building

"Form follows function"

People around the world have always admired tall buildings. For hundreds of years, cities throughout Europe were built around the stone spires of a church or cathedral. These buildings stretched upward and seemed to point the way to God and heaven.

But by the 19th century, the Industrial Revolution* was changing the way cities looked, especially in the United States. Places like New York and Chicago were growing rapidly. People from farms and small towns were moving there to find work in factories, department stores, and other businesses. The cities were growing so fast, in fact, that there was less and less land in the city center—where people wanted to work—for building new factories and office buildings. To solve this problem, city architects asked themselves how they could design a large structure that wouldn't take up much space on the ground, where land was scarce and valuable. The solution: build taller! Instead of having one company next door to another company, they could be on different floors of the same building. This arrangement enabled cities to house a growing number of workers, even in the most cramped, expensive downtown areas.

But making a tall building wasn't easy. As structures become higher and higher, strong winds, earthquakes, and other natural forces are more likely to damage them and even make them collapse. So the first skyscraper architects had to come up with a new kind of tall building that was both safe and durable. They solved this problem by

About This Building …

Date
  1896
Place
  Buffalo, New York, USA
Style
  Early modern
Height
  167 feet (51 meters)
Floors
  13
Designer
  Louis Sullivan

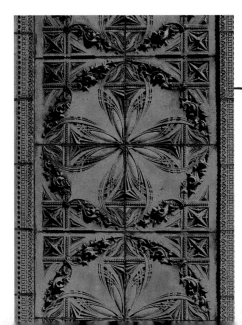

Elegant decoration

Louis Sullivan loved to design fancy ornaments. The Guaranty Building is covered with terra-cotta* blocks that feature Sullivan's complex designs, which look somewhat like sprouting plants.

5

Home Insurance Building

The skyscraper era began with architect William Le Baron Jenney's Home Insurance Building in Chicago. It was the first building to use a steel-frame skeleton. This new type of construction made tall buildings lighter and more durable. Just a few decades after the Home Insurance Building was completed in 1885, architects could use steel frames to design skyscrapers more than 100 stories high.

using a new kind of material: steel. Steel was strong and flexible, and it could resist the power of strong winds. Architects found that they could make a sturdy, tall building around a steel "frame," or skeleton. These frames were so sturdy, in fact, that the new office towers could have large windows, allowing people who worked in them to receive more light—and get beautiful views of the city from above! Other 19th-century inventions were also necessary to build a true skyscraper. Elevators enabled people to quickly travel up and down, for example. Indoor bathrooms were installed on every floor. And electric lights made it possible to work in even the darkest corners of the building.

For some architects, however, the skyscraper needed to be more than just a marvel of technology. They wanted to make buildings that were as beautiful as they were practical. One of the loveliest early skyscrapers is the Guaranty Building (now called the Prudential Building) in Buffalo, New York. Its architect, Louis Sullivan, believed that a building's "form" (its outward appearance) should reveal its "function" (what was going on inside the building). Sullivan covered the Guaranty Building with beautifully decorated blocks of terra-cotta,* but he did so in a way that reveals the form of the steel skeleton underneath. The tower's elegant piers* stretch upward toward the arches on top. Looking at the Guaranty Building from the outside, you can almost feel yourself going up in one of its elevators! Louis Sullivan's tower may not be the tallest of skyscrapers, but it was one of the first to make people feel they could truly work up in the sky.

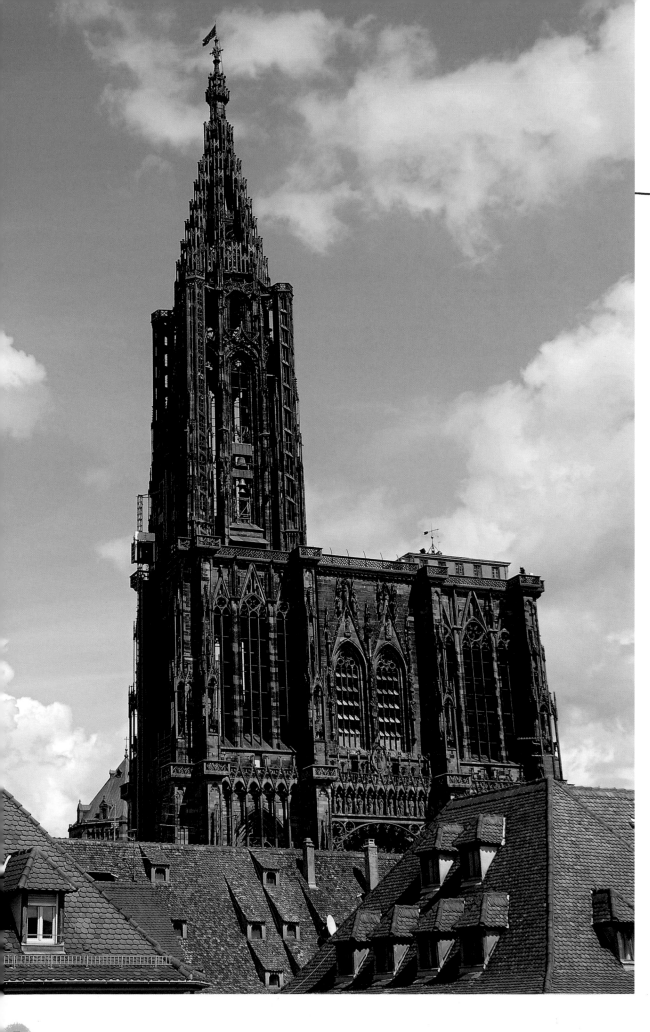

Tower of Strasbourg Cathedral

Some of the earliest "skyscrapers" in Europe were the elegant stone towers of cathedrals. This tower is from the cathedral in Strasbourg, France, completed in 1439. At 466 feet (142 meters) in height, it was the world's tallest building for more than 200 years—from 1647 (when a taller cathedral tower burned down) to 1874. Many "true" skyscrapers of the 1920s and '30s were built to look somewhat like Gothic* church towers.

Did you know?
One of Louis Sullivan's first apprentices was the young Frank Lloyd Wright, who went on to become America's most famous modern architect. You'll see more of Wright later in this book!

Woolworth Building

The Woolworth Building was among the first skyscrapers to truly soar over New York City. At 57 floors high and topped by a pointed crown, it looks like a super-sized cathedral tower!

Don't miss …
If you visit the Woolworth Building, be sure to see the beautiful lobby. Its walls are covered in marble, and it has a glittering mosaic* ceiling —almost like an ancient church!

❋ 1878 F. W. Woolworth opens his first store

❋ 1883 Brooklyn Bridge
completed in New York City

❋ 1898 Spanish-American War

❋ 1902 American inventor Willis
Carrier develops modern
air-conditioning

❋ 1914–18 World War I

875   1880   1885   1890   1895   1900   1905   1910   1915   1920   1925   1930

Woolworth Building

Reaching new heights

About This Building ...

Date
1910–13
Place
New York City, USA
Style
Gothic Revival*
Height
792 feet
(241 meters)
Floors
57
Designer
Cass Gilbert

For many people, early skyscrapers like the Guaranty Building don't look much like real towers. They are only ten or fifteen floors high, and they often seem to be hidden by newer, much taller buildings. The first truly massive skyscrapers were built in America's grandest city, New York—and the best known of these is the Woolworth Building.

Frank Winfield Woolworth was one of the wealthiest businessmen in the United States. He built "Woolworth" stores across America, which pro-vided people with clothes, tools, and other everyday items. Stores like Woolworth's changed the way people shopped. Instead of buying from local stores run by people in town, they now began to buy from "chain" stores that offered the same goods at lower prices.
This new kind of business required a new kind of building: a corporate headquarters* that controlled the activities of all the company's stores around the country.

F. W. Woolworth felt his head-quarters should stand out from all the other businesses in New York. So in 1910, he hired the architect Cass Gilbert to design

Medieval style

Cass Gilbert designed the Woolworth Building with Gothic*-style decoration over the windows and piers.*

a building far taller than any built before. Gilbert's Woolworth tower had to be constructed in several different sections. The first 30 floors of the building provide a stable base, above which stretches a thin, elegant tower. Gilbert designed the top of the tower to resemble a medieval Gothic* spire. And as Louis Sullivan did with the Guaranty Building, Gilbert used tall, thin piers* to make the tower look like it is stretching up toward the sky. At 57 stories and 792 feet (241 meters) in height, the Woolworth Building towered over all the other buildings in New York. And its elegant spire became a landmark that could be seen from miles away, helping to create a new kind of city skyline—one that celebrated American industry rather than God or religion. The Woolworth also enabled New Yorkers to see their city from a new perspective. From the building's vast number of windows (about 5,000 in all), visitors could get a true bird's-eye view of their growing metropolis. The Woolworth Building remained the tallest in the world for almost 20 years, from 1913 to 1930!

**Building an
early skyscraper**

This photo and the one on the opposite page show how an early skyscraper—the Flatiron Building in New York—was constructed. First, the steel skeleton was erected. Then, the builders would "cover" the skeleton with stone or other materials. In this picture, you can see how some of the floors have not yet received their "coat" of stone!

Flatiron Building

Although Chicago was the birthplace of the skyscraper, by 1900 New York City had become the center of the skyscraper-building world. The Flatiron Building was the first New York tower to become famous around the world. Designed by a Chicago architect named Daniel Burnham, this 20-story tower fits neatly into its triangular-shaped lot. Because of this shape, the Flatiron Building's appearance changes depending on where you look at it. If you view it from the side, it looks wide and massive. But if you view it from the front of its curved corner, it seems extremely thin. This photo shows the Flatiron Building while it was still under construction.

Tribune Tower

A worldwide design competition

About This Building …

Date
1923–25
Place
Chicago, Illinois, USA
Style
Gothic Revival*
Height
462 feet
(141 meters)
Floors
36
Designer
John Mead Howells
and Raymond Hood

By the 1920s, skyscrapers had become a world-famous symbol of the United States and its way of life. Architects from around the world were fascinated by American culture, and they began designing their own skyscrapers—even though most countries could not afford to build skyscrapers at that time. So when the *Chicago Tribune* newspaper company announced an international design competition for their new headquarters in 1922, they received designs from architects in Germany, Finland, Austria, and many other nations. Some of the designs were completely new. German architect Walter Gropius, who ran a modern art school called the Bauhaus, designed a tower of glass and steel without any fancy decoration. Other designs were more humorous. Austrian architect Adolf Loos's design resembled a huge Doric column* from an ancient Greek temple!

But the design that won the competition was much more conservative than these other plans. The American architects John Mead Howells and Raymond Hood devised a building that looked much like the Woolworth tower, with a Gothic-style spire resting on top of a larger base. Many architects, including Louis Sullivan, were upset with this choice. They wanted the *Tribune* to build a more daring tower—one that would reflect Chicago's very modern, fast-paced way of life.

A newspaper palace

The Tribune Tower became a mighty symbol of the *Chicago Tribune* newspaper.

1885 First skyscraper
built in Chicago

1893 Chicago World's Fair

1914–18 World War I

1919 Bauhaus art school
founded in Germany

1929 Stock market
crash in New York

885   1890   1895   1900   1905   1910   1915   1920   1925   1930   1935   1940

Tribune Tower

Like the Woolworth
Building, the Tribune
Tower reminds people
of a giant medieval
church tower. Its top
floors were designed
to resemble an elegant
crown of stone!

A Tribune column!

Some architects had fun with their designs for the Tribune Tower competition. Adolf Loos's skyscraper is actually a huge Doric column,* similar to the columns seen on ancient Greek temples. Loos knew his design would be impossible to build, but perhaps he wanted to make a humorous comment about American skyscrapers of the time, which were often made to look like historic buildings.

But despite these critics, the Tribune Tower has become just as famous a landmark in Chicago as the Woolworth Building is in New York. The tower offers visitors an unusual sight on its lower walls. Bits and pieces of ancient buildings from around the world have been stuck into these walls. Next

A modern tower

Walter Gropius's design for the Tribune Tower is very different from the winning design by Howells and Hood. Gropius helped develop the modern International Style* of architecture. International Style buildings are made of simple shapes and modern materials. After World War II ended in 1945, Gropius's style of building would become popular around the world, while buildings like Howells and Hood's Tribune Tower would be considered old-fashioned.

Good to know!
Many of the historic stone fragments on the Tribune Tower's lower walls come from delicate, ancient buildings like the Taj Mahal in India and the Parthenon in Greece. Today, it is illegal to take pieces of ancient buildings as souvenirs.

to each fragment, a small plaque describes where it came from and how old it is. *Chicago Tribune* reporters had traveled all over the world to cover important news stories, and the fragments tell visitors a little bit about those travels.

Chrysler Building

A skyscraper for the automobile age

In the Roaring Twenties, as the 1920s are sometimes called, the lives of ordinary people were changed forever. Americans in particular became wealthier than ever before, and they found new ways to entertain themselves. Jazz music, the radio, and motion pictures all became hugely popular. The way people dressed also changed, as women threw away their traditional clothes—which were stiff and heavy—and began wearing lighter, more comfortable outfits. But the most important change in American life may have been the automobile. Cars had been around since the late 1800s, but it wasn't until the 1920s that large numbers of people could afford to buy them. America's city streets were now filled with the sounds of roaring engines.

One man who helped create the automobile age was Walter P. Chrysler. He introduced his Chrysler automobile in 1924, and it soon became one of America's most popular cars. By 1928, the Chrysler Corporation had become so wealthy that it decided to build a grand new skyscraper for its headquarters in New York City. But Chrysler didn't want his building to resemble architecture from the past, like the Woolworth tower did. He wanted his building to reflect the modern American age. So his architect, William Van Alen, designed a tower in the sleek new Art Deco* style. As with most Art Deco buildings, the Chrysler tower featured elegant, rounded shapes and beautiful materials. You can see this most clearly in the building's spire, in which a series of round arches are placed on top of each other. The arches are covered in gleaming

About This Building …

Date
1928–30
Place
New York City, USA
Style
Art Deco*
Height (wth spire)
1,046 feet (319 meters)
Floors
77
Designer
William Van Alen

Elevator door in the Chrysler Building lobby

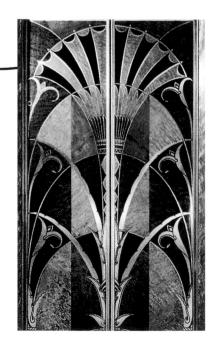

Walter P. Chrysler spared no expense in building his New York skyscraper. Every detail of the tower was beautifully made, even the elevator doors! The door shown here uses fancy inlaid wood marquetry* to create an elegant, plant-like design. Mr. Chrysler's employees could enjoy these elevators every morning when they arrived at work.

16

1908 Henry Ford develops the Model T car

1925 Chrysler Corporation founded

1927 First non-stop flight across the Atlantic

1939–45 World War II

1914–18 World War I

1929 Beginning of the Great Depression*

905   1910   1915   1920   1925   1930   1935   1940   1945   1950   1955   1960

steel, resembling the shiny decorations on Chrysler's automobiles.

The Chrysler Building would become part of a building boom in New York—one where different companies and builders competed against each other to erect the tallest building in the world. At 77 stories high, the Chrysler building was the world's tallest when it was completed in 1930. But it would remain so for only one year—as you'll learn in the next chapter!

Chrysler Building

The fancy crown of the Chrysler Building is a series of steel-clad arches, one on top of the other. These arches often remind people of the wheels and rounded shapes of Walter P. Chrysler's famous automobile.

The Chrysler building is famous for its funny gargoyles.* Instead of resembling the stone gargoyles from medieval churches, these sculptures are made of metal and look like hood ornaments, hub caps, and other parts of Chrysler automobiles. Try drawing your own skyscraper. How would you decorate it?

1857 Central Park opens
in New York City

1885 First skyscraper
built in Chicago

1893 Inventor Thomas Edison
sets up America's first movie studio

1855   1860   1865   1870   1875   1880   1885   1890   1895   1900   1905   191

Empire State Building

From a distance, the Empire State Building looks like it was made from a bunch of huge building blocks! These simple, rectangular shapes were popular during the Art Deco* period of architecture.

914–18
World War I

1933 The film *King Kong* is released

1929 Stock market
crash in New York

1937 *Hindenburg* airship* crashes

1939 New York World's Fair
1939–45
World War II

1945 United Nations established in New York

915   1920   1925   1930   1935   1940   1945   1950   1955   1960   1965   1970

Empire State Building

A beacon of light in the Great Depression

Even before the Chrysler Building was completed in 1930, a newer, much taller skyscraper was already going up in New York City. This new building was sponsored by two of the most powerful men in New York: business-man John J. Raskob and politician Alfred E. Smith. Smith had recently served as governor of New York, and he and Raskob wanted to build a tower that would represent more than just one company, as the Chrysler Building and the Woolworth tower did. They wanted a tower that would symbolize all of New York: the "Empire State."

In 1929, Smith and Raskob asked their architects—William F. Lamb and Richmond H. Shreve—to design a building that would stand as the world's tallest for many years. And what's more, they needed it to be built in only two years! Lamb designed the tower in the popular Art Deco* style, the same style as the Chrysler Building. However, it was up to Shreve to plan the huge build-ing's construction. So he and his team came up with several new ideas. First, they would hire more than 3,000 construction workers, far more than had ever been used on a skyscraper. They were able to do this, in part, because the United States econ-omy had changed. The New York stock market had crashed, businesses were losing money, and many people were out of

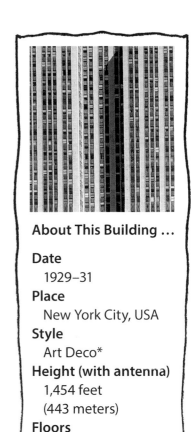

About This Building …

Date
1929–31
Place
New York City, USA
Style
Art Deco*
Height (with antenna)
1,454 feet
(443 meters)
Floors
102
Designer
William F. Lamb

A steel frame for the Empire State Building

As with earlier sky-scrapers, construction of the Empire State Building began by making a giant steel frame.

A working village in the sky

Construction workers had many different jobs to do on the Empire State Building. Some assembled the steel girders that made up the skyscraper's frame (above), while others prepared concrete and other building materials (below). All of these jobs took place hundreds of feet off the ground!

work. New York needed an exciting project to keep people's spirits up, and the Empire State Building was just such a project, hiring workers who might otherwise have remained unemployed.

Shreve also came up with other ideas for speeding up the tower's construction. For example, as the building went up, cafeterias were built on several stories to provide workers with food. A doctor and nurse were also on-site in case of injury. These features meant that workers wouldn't need to leave the site and slow down the building process. When completed in 1931, the Empire State truly "towered" over all New York. It was the first building to rise more than 100 stories, a record that would not be broken for almost 40 years. The tower also featured colorful electric lights on its spire, a bright image of hope in a country mired in the Great Depression.*

Quiz
The top floor and spire of the Empire State Building were originally designed as a kind of airport. Can you guess what this "airport" might have been for?

(Answer on page 46)

High up on the Empire State Building

Hang on tight! Photographer Lewis Hine captured this worker "flying" over New York City as he helped construct the Empire State Building. Hine thought the man resembled Icarus, a mythological character who soared toward the sun on man-made wings. Hundreds of workers such as this one risked their lives to construct the world's tallest skyscraper.

About This Building ...

Date
1957
Place
Moscow, Russia
(then the Soviet
Union)
Style
Stalinist neoclassical*
Height (with spire)
676 feet (206 meters)
Floors
34
Designer
Arkady Mordvinov

How would you design your own hotel? What shape would it be, and what colors and decorations would you use? Using building blocks or crayons, try making a miniature hotel for yourself, the more imaginative the better!

Hotel Ukraina

The skyscraper comes to Moscow

For many decades, skyscrapers were a luxury that few countries other than the United States could afford. But after World War II ended in 1945, a new superpower nation emerged: the Soviet Union. Soon, a new kind of war began between the Soviet Union and the United States. This "Cold War" didn't often involve battles. Instead, the two superpowers did all they could to show that their country had the better way of life. In the late 1940s, Soviet leader Joseph Stalin decided that America should not have a monopoly on skyscrapers. So he commissioned his architects to design and build a group of seven towers in the Soviet capital, Moscow. These towers, known today as the "Seven Sisters," were to display the success and wealth of his country.

Unlike the United States, the economy of the Soviet Union was Communist*—that is, it was run by the government and not by private businesses. Because the Soviet government had so much power, it could hire as many workers as it needed to build the new skyscrapers in Moscow. Stalin could also decide how the buildings should be used. Some towers would house government offices, while another would house the national university. But one of the most interesting towers was designed as a hotel: the Hotel Ukraina.

Like the other Seven Sisters, the Hotel Ukraina was built in a traditional style that Stalin preferred. It featured a tall spire that looked like part of a neoclassical* church, as well as columns and other details normally found on classical buildings. The lower part of the hotel was much wider than the top part, making it look a little like a giant wedding cake! When the Hotel Ukraina and the other Seven Sisters were completed in the late 1950s,

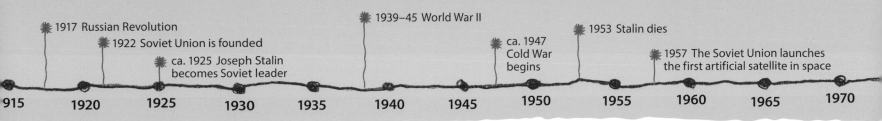

1917 Russian Revolution
1922 Soviet Union is founded
ca. 1925 Joseph Stalin becomes Soviet leader
1939–45 World War II
ca. 1947 Cold War begins
1953 Stalin dies
1957 The Soviet Union launches the first artificial satellite in space

915 1920 1925 1930 1935 1940 1945 1950 1955 1960 1965 1970

Stalin had already died. His towers gave Moscow a brand-new skyline, one quite different from most other cities in Europe and America. What's more, the Hotel Ukraina would remain the tallest hotel in the world until 1976! Today, the Soviet Union is long gone. But the people of Moscow, Russia, still admire their city's classical "sisters."

Hotel Ukraina

At night, the Hotel Ukraina looks like a gleaming, multi-colored palace.

Ludwig Mies van der Rohe 1881–1969

1871 Germany becomes a unified country

1889 The Eiffel Tower is built in Paris

1919 Bauhaus art school founded

1914–18 World War I

1865 1870 1875 1880 1885 1890 1895 1900 1905 1910 1915 192

About This Building …

Date
1954–58
Place
New York City, USA
Style
International Style*
Height
516 feet (157 meters)
Floors
38
Designer
Ludwig Mies van
der Rohe and
Philip Johnson

Seagram Building

A work of art in glass and steel

From the earliest years of the skyscraper, architects wanted to build a tower of glass. German architect Ludwig Mies van der Rohe designed such a sky-scraper for Berlin in 1922. It was a completely modern building, using modern materials and simple shapes instead of old-fashioned, fancy decoration. But as with many early ideas, this plan was too expensive and too difficult to build at the time.

After the National Socialists (the Nazis) took control of Germany in 1933, Mies decided to leave his home country and move to the United States. The Nazis didn't like modern art, and Mies felt he could teach his style of architecture more freely in America. So he moved to Chicago in 1938, where he taught at the Illinois Institute of Technology. Mies also began designing glass towers that were practical enough to be built. The most famous of these structures was a striking steel and glass tower created for the Seagram Company, which produced whiskey and other expensive alcoholic drinks.

Mies's 1922 design for a glass skyscraper

Mies's early designs for glass towers, such as this one from 1922, looked much brighter and more transparent than the buildings he designed in America. Mies also experimented with different shapes. This early design has curved walls, almost making it resemble a growing plant.

The Seagram Building was designed as a perfect rectangular box rising up from the city floor. At first, the dark exterior seems to be made completely of glass. But if you look closely, you can see steel beams in between each glass panel—beams that stretch upward to the top of the building. At the base of the tower, the building appears to rest on thin, rectangular steel columns. But this is all an illusion! The building is actually supported by a shaft made of concrete and steel which is hidden in the middle of the building.

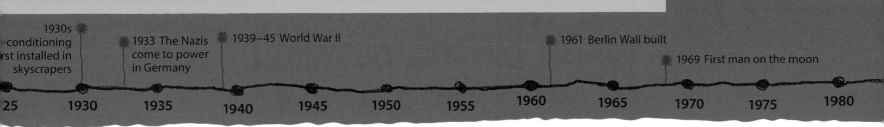

1930s air-conditioning first installed in skyscrapers

1933 The Nazis come to power in Germany

1939–45 World War II

1961 Berlin Wall built

1969 First man on the moon

25 1930 1935 1940 1945 1950 1955 1960 1965 1970 1975 1980

Despite the simple shape of the Seagram Building, Mies designed the tower in ways that made it look beautiful—especially when seen up close. The steel beams were coated with a layer of bronze, making the building shine in the sunlight. He also set the building back from the street and created a little plaza (or city park) in front of it. This plaza became one of the most popular places in New York City to sit, talk with other people, and sip a coffee. Mies's Seagram Building remains one of the most beautiful modern skyscrapers in the world, and many of the techniques used to build the structure are now used for all new towers.

Seagram Building

From a certain angle, the Seagram Building seems to float above the ground. Its massive concrete core,* which supports the building, is hidden inside the glass and steel walls.

Good to know

By the 1950s, many skyscrapers were becoming fully air-conditioned. This technology made the buildings much more comfortable in the summer. It also encouraged people to spend less time outside on the city streets and more time working indoors.

Fun fact

Even the Seagram Building's restaurant, called the Four Seasons, was designed to be a work of art. Mark Rothko, a famous American painter, was commissioned to decorate the restaurant with his artworks. But after completing the paintings in his studio, Rothko decided not to put them in the restaurant after all. He didn't feel people could appreciate his art while they were eating dinner! These paintings now hang in different museums around the world.

1886 Sears, Roebuck
and Company founded

1900 First *Wizard of Oz*
book published in Chicago

1914–18 World War I

1875   1880   1885   1890   1895   1900   1905   1910   1915   1920   1925   19

About This Building …

Date
 1970–73
Place
 Chicago, Illinois, USA
Style
 International Style*
Height
(without antennas)
 1,450 feet (442 meters)
Floors
 110
Designer
 Bruce Graham
 and Fazlur Khan
 (Skidmore,
 Owings & Merrill)

TransAmerica Pyramid

The Willis Tower was not the only sky-scraper of its day to "break out of the box." The TransAmerica Pyramid in San Francisco, California, is shaped like a skinny, four-sided pyramid—completely different from Mies van der Rohe's glass rectangles. Many modern skyscrapers are now designed with triangular shapes, which can increase the strength of their structures. You can read about two such buildings, the Shard in London and the One World Trade Center in New York, later in this book.

Willis Tower

Breaking out of the box

Mies van der Rohe's Seagram Building was so successful that in the 1950s and '60s, many cities decided to build their own glass-box towers. Few of these buildings were as beautiful as Mies's work, however. By the end of the 1960s, younger architects were looking for ways to "break out of the box" and design skyscrapers with more interesting, complex shapes.

In 1969, the world's largest department store chain, Sears, Roebuck and Company, needed a tower in Chicago where more than 300,000 employees could work. This tower would need to be bigger and taller than any ever built before. First, the company purchased two blocks of expensive downtown property, far more land than any previous skyscraper in Chicago had needed. Then they hired an architectural firm called Skidmore, Owings & Merrill (or SOM) to design a building 108 stories high!

SOM architect Bruce Graham and engineer Fazlur Khan developed a radical design for the new Sears Tower. They had seen an advertise-ment for a packet of cigarettes, where differ-ent cigarettes were shown sticking up out of the package at different heights. This image inspired them to create a building made of nine different shafts, or tubes,* that were also of different heights. By building this way, the structure of the Sears Tower would become extremely strong and resist the powerful winds that blow 100 floors above the ground. This structure also enabled SOM to make the tower look like a new kind of modern sky-

1936 Skidmore, Owings & Merrill founded

1939–45
World War II

late 1940s Television becomes
popular in the USA

ca. 1947 Cold War begins

1964 The Beatles rock
band first tours the USA

1969 First man
on the moon

1975 First personal
computers become popular

1935　　1940　　1945　　1950　　1955　　1960　　1965　　1970　　1975　　1980　　1985　　1990

Willis Tower

The rectangular shafts, or tubes,* of the Willis Tower rise upward at different levels. These tubes make the building's overall structure much stronger, enabling the tower to support 110 floors!

Don't miss …
Visitors to the Willis Tower can take an elevator to the famous "Skydeck" for a bird's-eye view of the city. In 2009, enclosed glass balconies were added to the Skydeck. If you're brave enough, you can walk out on a balcony and look straight down to the city street—1,300 feet below your shoes!

scraper, one that almost seemed to be breaking apart at the top and reaching for the clouds. Now known as the Willis Tower, this building remains the mightiest building in a city of skyscrapers—a giant cigarette packet in the sky.

b. 1926 César Pelli

1942–45 Japan controls
Kuala Lumpur

1955–75 Vietnam War

1939–45 World War II

1950–53
Korean War

| 1900 | 1905 | 1910 | 1915 | 1920 | 1925 | 1930 | 1935 | 1940 | 1945 | 1950 | 19 |

Petronas Towers

Twin giants in Malaysia

Beginning in the 1970s, skyscraper building spread all around the world. Many nations wanted their towers to be distinctive, often with unusual shapes and materials. And by the 1990s, a few Asian cities were becoming rich enough to think about building skyscrapers even taller than the highest American towers.

One such city was Kuala Lumpur, capital of the Southeast Asian country of Malaysia. In the 1980s, oil and trade had brought Malaysia new wealth. So in 1990, Malaysia's national oil company decided to build a monument to its growing nation. After holding a worldwide design competition, it chose the Argentinean-born architect César Pelli. Pelli's design featured two towers connected by a thin walkway. These buildings have a shape that reminds many people in Malaysia of their national religion, Islam. If you look at the towers from above, they each resemble an eight-pointed star. Pelli chose this shape because it comes from ancient Islamic architecture.*

About This Building ...

Date
1993–96
Place
Kuala Lumpur,
Malaysia
Style
Postmodern*
Height
1,483 feet
(452 meters)
Floors
88
Designer
César Pelli

Marina City

The Petronas Towers were not the first skyscrapers to have rounded bodies. In 1959, architect Bertram Goldberg designed circular twin towers in Chicago. Made of reinforced concrete,* the Marina City towers were a new type of apartment building. Many people in America at that time had moved away from the city and bought homes in the suburbs. Marina City was designed to make people want to live downtown again. The towers provided residents with almost everything they would need: restaurants, stores, parking lots, and a theater and other places for entertainment. Today, many downtown apartment towers offer these kinds of benefits, as more and more people decide to live in the city.

The Petronas Towers are designed as a series of shafts, or tubes,* placed one on top of the other. Similar to the tubes in the Sears Tower, these shafts gradually get smaller the higher up they go. Pelli also used polished steel and glass on the outside of the buildings, giving the

28

7 Malaysia becomes independent
he Federation of Malaya

1974 Petronas oil and gas
company founded

1989
Fall of the
Berlin Wall

1991 The Soviet Union breaks apart

2007
First iPhone

1960   1965   1970   1975   1980   1985   1990   1995   2000   2005   2010   2015

Petronas Towers

The twin spires of Kuala Lumpur's Petronas Towers are connected by a thin walking bridge. The buildings' architect, César Pelli, used this bridge to form a kind of arch … a "gateway" that would lead visitors into Malaysia's modern capital city.

towers a much shinier, brighter appearance than earlier modern skyscrapers. According to Pelli, the Petronas Towers were meant to resemble a giant gate leading visitors into a new city. When lit up at night, they sparkle like jewels in the warm Malaysian sky.

Learn more
You can read more about the Petronas Towers and other famous tall buildings in *Skyscrapers,* by Andres Lepik.

About This Building ...

Date
2004–09
Place
Dubai, United
Arab Emirates
Style
Neo-futurist*
Height
2,722 feet (830 meters)
Floors
154
Designer
Adrian Smith
(Skidmore, Owings
& Merrill)

Fun fact
The Burj Khalifa has one
of the highest outdoor
swimming pools in the
world. People can take a
dip on the building's 76th
floor—a real luxury in the
middle of the desert!

Quiz
What does the name
Burj Khalifa mean?
(Answer on page 46)

Burj Khalifa

Above the desert and into the clouds

Over the last 40 years, the city of Dubai has changed more than almost any other place on Earth. For centuries, Dubai was a small coastal town in the Arabian desert—known mostly for its fishermen and the beautiful pearls that came from the nearby Persian Gulf. But the discovery of oil in the 1960s brought unimaginable wealth to this small place. By 1971, Dubai had become a growing city in a new nation called the United Arab Emirates.

Dubai's leaders soon began hiring architects from around the world to completely rebuild their city. The old, narrow city streets with their whitewashed houses were demolished, replaced by wide boulevards and gleaming new skyscrapers. By the early 2000s, the old fishing village had a skyline as large as many cities in Europe and North America. But Dubai's leaders wanted something more. They wanted their city to have a skyscraper that would dwarf any other tower on Earth. So they hired an architectural firm that had already designed one of the tallest buildings in the world. Do you remember Skidmore, Owings & Merrill (SOM)? They were the architects of the mighty Sears Tower in Chicago.

For the new Burj Khalifa, SOM used some of the same ideas it developed for the Sears Tower. For example, the Dubai tower is designed as a bundle of tubes* which extend upwards to different heights. But instead of the rectangular-shaped tubes seen in the Sears Tower, the Burj Khalifa's tubes are rounded. The architects also developed a newer, stronger concrete core* to support the building. If you could look at the core from above, you'd see that it's shaped like a curving letter "Y." Together, the curved tubes and Y-shaped core help reduce the damaging effects of wind and keep the building stable. Stability, of course, is the most important feature of any tall building. And what a giant the Burj Khalifa is: it stands 2,722 feet (830 meters) high,

1969 First man
on the moon

1966 Oil
discovered
in Dubai

1971 Dubai
becomes part of
the United Arab
Emirates

1979 Iranian Revolution

1990–91 Persian Gulf War

2001 United
States attacked on
September 11

2015 First space-
craft to fly by the
dwarf planet Pluto

1960   1965   1970   1975   1980   1985   1990   1995   2000   2005   2010   2015

with more than 150 floors. The Burj is so much taller than its neighboring buildings in Dubai that it almost looks unreal in photographs—a modern mirage in the Arabian desert.

Burj Khalifa

Looking like a bundle of tree trunks, the Burj Khalifa seems to pierce the desert sky.

Mile-High Skyscraper

The Burj Khalifa may be tall, but in 1956, American architect Frank Lloyd Wright designed a building that would stand a mile (1,600 meters) high—twice as tall as the tower in Dubai. Wright's skyscraper, called the Mile High Illinois, would have included parking places for 150 helicopters! Unfortunately, the design was never built. But some of Wright's ideas were later used by other architects. The triangular shape of the base is similar to the concrete core of the Burj Khalifa. Wright also figured out that an extremely tall building needs to gradually become smaller and narrower as it rises. Today, many architects believe that a mile-high skyscraper similar to Wright's design could actually be built!

1904 Scottish author
J. M. Barrie writes
the play *Peter Pan*

1914–18 World War I

1939–45 World War II

b. 1937 Renzo Piano

ca. 1947
Cold War begins

1953 Queen
Elizabeth II
is crowned

1900 1905 1910 1915 1920 1925 1930 1935 1940 1945 1950 195

The Shard

A modern spire in historic London

About This Building …

Date
2009–12
Place
London,
United Kingdom
Style
Neo-futurist*
Height
1,004 feet
(306 meters)
Floors
95
Designer
Renzo Piano

London is a place of history. More than 2,000 years old, the city has long been a home for Britain's kings and queens, artists and writers, and prime ministers and business tycoons. London's history is also reflected in its historic buildings: its mighty cathedrals, elegant palaces and classical museums. Londoners have always admired their traditional architecture, and for much of the twentieth century they wanted to keep the "look" of their city as it was … without any modern skyscrapers. Until 1962, in fact, London's tallest building was the centuries-old St. Paul's cathedral!

Since the late 1900s, however, the city's appearance has changed dramatically. Much of London is now dominated by elegant glass towers, some of which

The Shard

Finished in 2012, the Shard rises elegantly over the River Thames in London. The building's shape may remind you of another skyscraper in this book: the TransAmerica Pyramid in San Francisco (see page 26). Both towers have a pyramid-like appearance that makes them stand out from the other landmarks in their city.

1960 *The Beatles* rock band is founded

1982 Falklands War between Argentina and Great Britain

1991 Cold War ends

2011 Prince William marries Katherine Middleton

1997 First *Harry Potter* book is published

1960 1965 1970 1975 1980 1985 1990 1995 2000 2005 2010 2015

The Gherkin

Like the Shard, the pickle-shaped "Gherkin" has become a famous symbol of modern London. Designed by British architect Norman Foster, it replaced a group of historic buildings that had been destroyed by terrorists* in 1992. Foster's tower uses clever ways of bringing natural light and air into the tower, enabling people who work there to use less artificial light and air conditioning. These features make the skyscraper a kind of "green" building — one that helps reduce the amount of water, oil and other resources that people take from the environment.

have quite unusual shapes. One such skyscraper is nicknamed "the Gherkin" because it resembles a giant pickle! But the tallest and most dramatic of these modern buildings—the Shard—has a shape that's meant to remind people of London's past.

The Shard was designed by a famous Italian architect named Renzo Piano. It features tall, elegant triangular walls of steel and glass. As with many skyscrapers, these walls are built around a concrete core, which gives the building strength and stability. When Piano first showed his designs to the public, some people were critical of them. They thought the building would resemble a giant "shard of glass through the heart of historic London." But as the structure was being built, Londoners began to realize how graceful Piano's tower really was. They saw how the glass walls could reflect light in different ways at different times of the day … making the building appear to change color as the sun rose and set. Many also saw the tower as a kind of modern-day cathedral spire, somewhat resembling the city's famous gothic* steeples. And though it would acquire "The Shard" as its official name, Piano's skyscraper has now become one of Britain's most admired landmarks. It seems to celebrate two things at once: London's ancient history and its role as a leading center of twenty-first-century business and trade.

Places to visit
If you travel to London, you'll have an easy time getting to the Shard. That's because the tower stands next to an important stop on the Tube, London's subway network. This site not only makes it easy for tourists to see the building, it also makes it easy for people who work in the tower to travel to and from their offices.

Glass and light

At sunset, the Shard begins to glow from within—as the lights inside its glassy walls become brighter against the darkening sky.

About This Building …

Date
2006–13
Place
New York City, USA
Style
Modern
Height (main building)
1,776 feet
(541 meters)
Floors
49
Designer
David Childs
(Skidmore, Owings
& Merrill)

One World Trade Center

A symbol of healing in
New York City

When people visited New York
before September 11, 2001, the
World Trade Center towers were
often the first landmark they
noticed. These "twin towers"
housed businesses from all over
the world, and they symbolized
the importance of New York as a
truly international city. So when
the buildings were destroyed
by al-Qaeda* terrorists* on
September 11—an attack that
killed almost 3,000 people—New
Yorkers knew they would have to
rebuild their damaged city. They
would also need to create a new
monument that could honor all
the lives that had been lost.

One World Trade Center

The reflective walls of
One World Trade Center
capture the colors of a
New York City sunset.

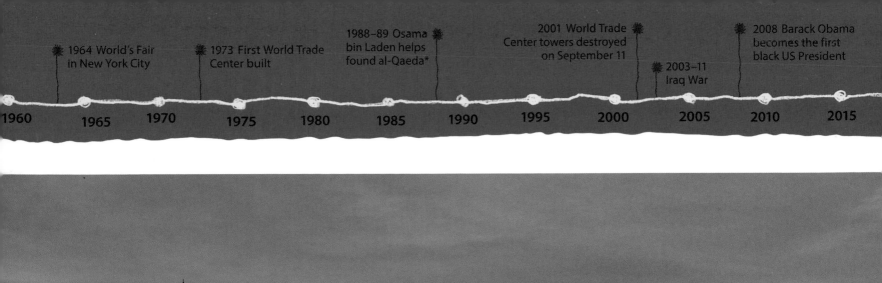

1964 World's Fair in New York City

1973 First World Trade Center built

1988–89 Osama bin Laden helps found al-Qaeda*

2001 World Trade Center towers destroyed on September 11

2003–11 Iraq War

2008 Barack Obama becomes the first black US President

1960   1965   1970   1975   1980   1985   1990   1995   2000   2005   2010   2015

The original World Trade Center buildings

The original World Trade Center towers were designed by a Japanese-American architect named Minoru Yamasaki. When completed in 1971, the towers' plain, simple, modern style was going out of fashion, and many people found them ugly. But no one believed that such sturdy, well-designed buildings could be destroyed by the actions of two airplanes on 9/11.

At the top of New York

One World Trade Center is topped by a thin spire, which acts as an antenna.

In 2002, after the city received many ideas for how to rebuild the site, they decided to construct a single skyscraper as part of the new World Trade Center site. The final design of this tower was ready for building by 2005, and it was completed in 2013. Now called the One World Trade Center, it has a more complex shape than the rectangular towers that were destroyed on September 11. Beginning on the 20th floor, the outer walls of the tower form eight skinny triangles. This shape, along with the steel and glass panels that cover the walls, makes the building look like a cut jewel or a prism. The triangular walls are like mirrors, each reflecting a different part of the surrounding sky and city.

One World Trade Center was designed to be especially stable. Not only does it have a concrete core* and other supports to prevent wind damage, but it also has a massive concrete structure underneath that protects the building from bombs and other terrorist activities that might occur in the future. But perhaps the most symbolic part of the tower is its size. The main part of the building stands exactly 1,776 feet high, in order to represent the year of American independence: 1776. This height also makes it the tallest building in all of North and South America. Today, visitors flock to the World Trade Center site to remember the events of 9/11. Those who go to One World Trade Center's observation deck on the 100th floor can look down on a city healed from the wounds it suffered in those events.

Learn more
To learn more about what happened on September 11, 2001, you can visit the National September 11 Memorial & Museum. It stands next to the One World Trade Center in New York City.

Shanghai Tower

A city within a skyscraper

About This Building …

Date
2008–15
Place
Shanghai, China
Style
Postmodern,*
Green architecture*
Height
2,073 feet
(632 meters)
Floors
128
Designer
Jun Xia (and the
Gensler architectural
firm)

Like Dubai, the city of Shanghai has been growing faster than almost any other place in the world. A center of China's vast economy, Shanghai has attracted people from all over the country to live and work there. So many people have moved to Shanghai in recent years, however, that the city has become overcrowded and polluted. What's more, the price of land in the downtown area has skyrocketed.

To address these problems, Shanghai's government and business leaders developed a plan to construct several new kinds of "megatall"* skyscrapers. These buildings serve the same basic purpose that the earliest skyscrapers did: providing new office space without taking up too much room on the ground in a place where land is very expensive. But one of Shanghai's new towers goes much further than that. Called the Shanghai Tower, its design makes it stand out from the other megatall structures in the city. The building was designed by a Chinese architect named Jun Xia, and it takes full advantage of all the latest skyscraper technology. Jun Xia and his assistants used computer programs to determine the building's shape and the way it was to be supported. Their final design was extremely complex. The inner part of the tower is divided into nine rounded tubes* placed one on top of the other. Covering the tubes is a curved, twisting outer wall of glass and steel. The shape of this outer wall almost looks like a coat twirled around a tall person in the wind. As with other modern skyscrapers we've seen in this book, the curving walls and tubes help prevent wind damage.

But what makes the Shanghai Tower so unusual is what happens on the inside. Jun Xia designed the outer wall so that it extends far out from the building's inner tubes. On each floor, the spaces between the tubes and the outer wall are used to create light-filled gardens, parks, restaurants, and

1976 Chinese leader
Mao Zedong dies

1978 China opens up
trade with the West

1991
Cold War
ends

1997 Hong Kong becomes
part of China

2008 Olympic Games
held in Beijing

2010 Shanghai's
population
reaches more
than 20 million

1960   1965   1970   1975   1980   1985   1990   1995   2000   2005   2010   2015

Shanghai Tower

The form of Shanghai
Tower twists like a
giant snake. This shape
makes the building more
stable and less likely to
be damaged by high
winds.

Quiz
As of 2015, the Shanghai
Tower's elevators traveled
faster and farther than
any other elevator in the
world. Can you guess how
fast and how far they go?
(Answer on page 46)

CCTV Headquarters*

Since 2000, many Chinese cities have become completely transformed by new and exciting skyscraper designs. This building houses China's government-run television company in Beijing. Designed by Dutch architect Rem Koolhaas, the CCTV Headquarters shows that a skyscraper doesn't need to have a tower shape. Koolhaas's design looks more like a piece of modern sculpture than a building. Nevertheless, it stands 768 feet (234 meters) high and has 44 stories!

other places to relax. People who work in the Shanghai Tower have their offices in the tower's central section. But when they need to take a break, they can simply walk out into a sun-filled park without ever having to leave the building! And because the outer walls keep out pollution from the city, these parks can be much healthier and more enjoyable than outdoor Shanghai. In addition, if the tower's businesses need to invite guests from abroad to work in the tower, part of the building can house a hotel for them. All of these features make the Shanghai Tower a kind of miniature city, with almost every convenience one would need in the outside world. As cities around the globe continue to grow and become more crowded, these kinds of skyscrapers may become more common—and more necessary.

Glossary

AIRSHIP is a kind of flying machine that, unlike an airplane, is lighter than air. The most famous airships were the huge, balloon-like flying zeppelins.

AL-QAEDA is a terrorist* organization founded, in part, by Osama bin Laden. This organization coordinated the tragic events of 9/11.

ART DECO, in architecture, is a style that uses elegant geometric shapes and often lavish materials such as marble and stained glass. Art Deco was especially popular in the 1920s and 1930s.

COMMUNISM is a political philosophy, or way of thinking, that was supported by many governments in the 1900s. In Communist countries, such as the former Soviet Union, most businesses and farms are controlled by the government. In capitalist countries, such as the United States, most businesses are controlled by people outside the government. China is one of the few Communist nations that exist today.

CORE, in skyscraper building, is a central shaft that often provides the chief support for the tower's structure. Such cores are often made of concrete and steel.

CORPORATE HEADQUARTERS is a building or other place where the leaders of a large company work.

DORIC COLUMN is a type of ancient Greek column that has a simple, flat capital (or top block).

GARGOYLE is a kind of water spout first used on medieval churches. Gargoyles are often carved in the form of strange animals. Their purpose is to help drain water from a building's roof.

GOTHIC is the name of a style of art common in Europe during the Middle Ages, from about 1200 to 1500. Gothic buildings often feature pointed arches and tall towers.

GOTHIC REVIVIAL is a style of art in which paintings, sculptures, and buildings are made to have a Gothic appearance. Gothic Revival architecture was especially popular in the 1800s and early 1900s.

GREAT DEPRESSION was a time, mostly during the 1930s, when businesses around the world lost money and many people were out of work.

GREEN ARCHITECTURE is a term used for buildings designed to save energy and use fewer precious resources from the environment—resources such as water and oil.

INDUSTRIAL REVOLUTION was a period in history when Europeans began making products in large factories with machines, instead of making them by hand. This period began in England in the 1700s.

INTERNATIONAL STYLE is an architectural style that uses modern industrial materials (such as steel and concrete) and angular shapes, while avoiding any traditional ornament. This style was most popular in the 1950s and 1960s.

ISLAMIC ARCHITECTURE is a building style related to cultures that practice the religion of Islam. These cultures include people from the Middle East, who developed a kind of architecture known for its pointed arches and elaborate decoration.

MARQUETRY is the art of making designs from carefully shaped pieces of wood and other materials. People often use marquetry to decorate doors and furniture.

MEGATALL is a term used for the extremely tall skyscrapers built since the 1990s.

MOSAIC is a kind of decoration using tiny pieces of colored stone. Mosaics often decorate the walls and ceilings of buildings.

NEOCLASSICAL, in architecture, is a style of building designed to look somewhat like the ancient structures of classical Greece and Rome.

NEO-FUTURIST, in architecture, is a modern style that uses new technology and unusual forms to create buildings that suggest future ways of living.

PIER, in skyscraper building, is a thin shaft that often forms part of the building's structure. Piers can be made of steel, concrete, or other materials.

POSTMODERNISM means "after modernism." Postmodern architects became famous for using arches, columns, and other historical forms that International Style* architects had avoided. These architects tended to criticize boxy modernist designs such as Mies van der Rohe's Seagram Building.

REINFORCED CONCRETE is a kind of concrete made stronger by the use of materials such as steel and plastic. Reinforced concrete is much more durable than regular concrete, and it is commonly used in modern skyscrapers.

SERFS were peasants who did not own their own land and had to work for wealthy, aristocratic families. . . somewhat like slaves in the United States. Serfs in Russia were not given their freedom until the 19th century.

TERRA-COTTA is a kind of baked clay that was once used to decorate the outsides of buildings. This material was durable, and architects could create beautiful decorations on it.

TERRORISTS commit acts of violence, such as the killing of innocent people, to achieve certain goals. Many terrorist acts are committed against certain countries or governments.

TUBE, in architecture, is the name for an individual shaft of a building. Some large skyscrapers are made of several tubes stacked one on top of the other.

WATER CLOSET is another name for a bathroom or toilet.

Answers to the Quiz Questions

Page 20:   The top of the Empire State Building was designed, in part, as a port for zeppelins and other airships.*
The airship would be tied to the spire, and the passengers would disembark onto the 103rd floor.
This "airport" didn't last long, however, as high winds at the top of the Empire State Building made
landing and exiting airships too dangerous.

Page 30:   The word "burj" means "tower" in Arabic, while the name "Khalifa" refers to Sheik Khalifa bin Zayed,
who was the leader of the United Arab Emirates when the Burj Khalifa was completed in 2009.

Page 41:   The Shanghai Tower's elevators can travel at more than 40 miles (64 kilometers) per hour. In total,
they travel almost 1,900 feet (578 meters) from bottom to top!

© Prestel Verlag, Munich · London · New York, 2016
A member of Verlagsgruppe Random House GmbH
Neumarkter Strasse 28 · 81673 Munich
© for the works held by the artists or their legal
heirs except for Frank Lloyd Wright: VG Bild-Kunst,
Bonn 2016

Prestel Publishing Ltd.
14-17 Wells Street
London W1T 3PD

Prestel Publishing
900 Broadway, Suite 603
New York, NY 10003

Photo Credits: Chicago Historical Society, Chicago:
p. 6; Chicago Tribune Tower Competition, vol. 1, New
York, 1981: pp. 14/15; CORBIS, Angelo Hornack: p. 2,
8/9; Thomas A. Heinz: pp. 2, 4/5; Esto, Mamaroneck,
Peter Mauss: pp. 2, 18/19; Frank Llyod Wright Founda-
tion, Scottsdale, AZ: p. 31; gettyimages, Bloomberg /
Kontributor: pp. 2, 12/13; Interim Archives / Kontributor: pp. 10/11; Mario Tama / Staff: pp. 2, 16/17, 44;
Max_Ryazanov: pp. 2, 22/23; MyLoupe / Kontributor:
pp. 5, 45; PATRICK HERTZOG / Staff: p. 7; Pawel Toczyn-
ski: pp. 2, 24/25; Richard l'Anson: pp. 2, 26/27; Zhang
Peng / Kontributor: pp. 2, 40/41, 45; IFA Bilderteam,
Munich, Travel Pixs: p. 38; Look-foto, age fotostock:
pp. 2, 3, 28/29, 30/31, 32/33, 45; Hauke Dressler: p. 26;
Photononstop: Schmutztitel, pp. 3, 36/37, 39; Nigel
Young/Foster + Partners: pp. 3, 34/35, 45; OMA Office
for Metropolitan Architecture, Rotterdam: pp. 42/43,
44; Scala, Florence / The Museum of Modern Art, New
York © 2004: p. 24

Front Cover: The Shard, London, UK (pp. 32/33)
Burj Khalifa, Dubai, United Arab Emirates (pp. 30/31)
Chrysler Building, New York, USA (Look-foto,
Torsten Andreas Hoffmann)

Frontispiece: Petronas Towers,
Kuala Lumpur, Malaysia (pp. 28/29)

Copyediting: Rita Forbes
Picture editor and project management: Mareike Rinke
Production management: Astrid Wedemeyer
Layout: Meike Sellier, Eching
Conceptual Design: Michael Schmölzl,
agenten.und.freunde, Munich
Separations: ReproLine Mediateam, Munich
Printing and Binding: Printer Trento, Trento
Paper: Hello Fat Matt

Verlagsgruppe Random House
FSC® N001967

ISBN 978-3-7913-7251–8
www.prestel.com